THE LAST CALL

By J.T.C.

Chick Publications, P.O. Box 662
Chino, CA 91708-0662 USA

Phone: (909) 987-0771 • Fax: (909) 941-8128

Business Offices: 8780 Archibald, Cucamonga, CA 91730

I wish to thank the Fleming H. Revell Company for permission to use a condensed portion of their great book "Revival Lectures" by Charles G. Finney, one of the most important books of our times.   J.T.C.

Christian, this booklet briefly sets forth the key for revival. Study it and put it into action in your own life and in your church.

The play period is over. If you are not interested in revival, you had better start looking for the sack-cloth and ashes — you may soon expect to see the following scenes become a reality.

REVIVAL OR MARTYRDOM

THE CHOICE IS YOURS,

THIS COULD INDEED BE . . .

"THE LAST CALL!"

100 years ago, God raised up a voice so cutting, that it penetrated the hardened hearts of the sleeping Churches. The Christians were shocked and angered by such piercing words. God was crushing the believers by the voice of Charles G. Finney and a tremendous revival swept over our land.

Today there is no voice strong enough to awaken the sleeping Christians and the end time is here.

The Lord has placed on my heart to bring before the believers some of Finney's burning words. May our Lord use them to spark a flaming revival. Our King is coming. Let us be found laboring at his appearing.

TABLE OF CONTENTS

What A Revival Is 5

When A Revival Is Needed 6

When A Revival May Be Expected 8

How To Promote A Revival 9

Prevailing Prayer 19

Prayer Of Faith 22

Spirit Of Prayer 23

On Being Filled With The Spirit 23

The Consequences Of Having The Fullness Of The Spirit .. 26

Meeting For Prayer 26

Testifying To The Unsaved 30

To Win Souls Requires Wisdom 32

A Wise Minister Will Be Successful 35

How To Preach The Gospel 36

How Can Churches Help Ministers 39

Hinderances To Revival 42

Necessity And Effect Of Union 47

False Comfort For Sinners 49

Directions To Sinners 51

Instructions To Converts 53

The Backslider In Heart 57

Growth In Grace 60

4

(Please note the text in this book is the work of
Charles G. Finney)

REVIVAL

WHAT A REVIVAL IS

A revival is nothing else than a believer's new beginning of obedience to God.

A revival always includes conviction of sin on the part of the Church. Backslidden professors cannot wake up and begin right away in the service of God, without deep searchings of heart. The fountains of sin need to be broken up. In a true revival, Christians are always brought under such conviction; they see their sins in such a light that often they find it impossible to maintain a hope of their acceptance with God.

Christians will have their faith renewed. While they are in their backslidden state they are blind to the state of sinners. Their hearts are hard as marble. The truths of the Bible appear like a dream. They admit it to be all true; their conscience and their judgment assent to it; but their faith does not see it standing out in bold relief, in all the burning realities of eternity. But when they enter into a revival, they no longer see "men as trees, walking," but they see things in that strong light which will renew the love of God in their hearts.   This will lead them to labour zealously to bring others to Him. They will feel grieved that others do not love God, when they love Him so much. And they will set themselves feelingly to persuade their neighbours to give Him their hearts. So their love to men will be renewed. They will be filled with a tender and burning love for souls. They will have a longing desire for the salvation of the whole world. They will be in an agony for individuals whom they want to have saved — their friends, relations, enemies. They will not only be urging them to give their hearts to God, but they will carry them to God in the arms of faith, and with strong crying and tears beseech God to have mercy on them, and save their souls from endless burnings.

When the Churches are thus awakened and reformed, the reformation and salvation of sinners will follow. Their hearts will be broken down and changed. Very often the most abandoned profiligates are among the subjects. Harlots, and drunkards, and infidels, and all sorts of abandoned characters, are awakened and converted. The worst of human beings are softened and reclaimed, and made to appear as lovely specimens of the beauty of holiness.

WHEN A REVIVAL IS NEEDED

When there is a want of brotherly love and Christian confidence among professors of religion, then a revival is needed.

When the wicked triumph over the Churches, and revile them, it is time to seek for a revival of religion.

A revival of religion is the only possible thing that can wipe away the reproach which covers the Church and restore religion to the place it ought to have in the estimation of the public. Without a revival, this reproach will cover the Church more and more, until it is overwhelmed with universal contempt. There must be a waking up of energy on the part of Christians, and an outpouring of God's Spirit, or the world will laugh at the Church.

At such a time a revival of religion is indispensable to avert the Judgments of God from the Church. This would be a strange preaching if revivals were only miracles, and if the Church has no more agency in producing them than it has in producing a thunderstorm. We could not then say to the Church: "Unless there is a revival you may expect Judgments." The fact is, Christians are more to blame for not being revived, than sinners are for not being converted. And if they are not awakened, they may know assuredly that God will visit them with His judgments.

Some people are terribly alarmed at all direct efforts to promote a revival, and they cry out: "You are trying to get up a revival in your own strength. Take care, you are interfering with the Sovereignty of God. Better keep along in the usual course, and let God give a revival when He thinks it is best. God is a Sovereign, and it is very wrong for you to attempt to get up a revival, just because you think a revival is needed." This is just such preaching as the devil wants. And men cannot do the devil's work more effectually than by preaching up the Sovereignty of God as a reason why we should not put forth efforts to produce a revival.

7

WHEN A REVIVAL MAY BE EXPECTED

When the wickedness of the wicked grieves and humbles and distresses Christians.

Look back over your past history. Take up your individual sins one by one, and look at them. I do not mean that you should just cast a glance at your past life, and see that it has been full of sins, and then go to God and make a sort of general confession, and ask for pardon. That is not the way. You must take them up one by one. It will be a good thing to take a pen and paper, as you go over them, and write them down as they occur to you. Go over them as carefully as a merchant goes over his books; and as often as a sin comes before your memory, add it to the list. General confessions of sin will never do. Your sins were committed one by one; and as far as you can come at them, they ought to be reviewed and repented of one by one.

When you have gone over your whole history in this way, thoroughly, if you will then go over the ground the second time, and give your solemn and fixed attention to it, you will find that the things you have put down will suggest other things of which you have been guilty, connected with them, or near them. Then go over it a third time, and you will recollect other things connected with these. And you will find in the end that you can remember an amount of history, and particular actions, even in this life, which you did not think you would remember in eternity. Unless you take up your sins in this way, and consider them in detail, one by one, you can form no idea of the amount of them. You should go over the list as thoroughly, and as carefully, and as solemnly, as you would if you were just preparing yourself for the Judgment.

9

CONSIDER THE FOLLOWING SINS

INGRATITUDE

SET DOWN THE INSTANCES OF GOD'S GOODNESS TO YOU WHEN YOU WERE IN SIN, BEFORE YOUR CONFESSION; FOR WHICH YOU HAVE NEVER BEEN HALF THANKFUL ENOUGH; AND THE NUMEROUS MERCIES YOU HAVE RECEIVED SINCE.

NEGLECT OF THE BIBLE

PERHAPS FOR WEEKS OR LONGER

NO WONDER YOUR RELIGION IS SUCH A MISERABLE FAILURE

10

UNBELIEF

I KNOW YOU PROMISED THE FILLING OF THE HOLY SPIRIT TO THEM THAT ASK YOU---BUT I REALLY DON'T BELIEVE IT!

IF YOU HAVE NOT BELIEVED NOR EXPECTED TO RECEIVE THE BLESSING WHICH GOD HAS EXPRESSLY PROMISED— YOU HAVE CHARGED HIM WITH LYING.

NEGLECT OF PRAYER

MECHANICAL, LAZY PRAYERS, WITHOUT FEELING

11

LACK OF LOVE FOR FRIENDS AND RELATIVES

WANT AND CARE FOR THE HEATHEN

BUT THAT'S THE MISSIONARY'S JOB, NOT MINE!

Perhaps you have not cared enough for them to attempt to learn their condition; perhaps not even to take a missionary magazine. Look at this, and see how much you really care for the heathen, and set down **12** honestly the real amount of your feelings for them, and your desire for their salvation. Measure your desire for their salvation by the self-denial you practice in giving of your substance to send them the Gospel. Do you deny yourself even the hurtful superfluities of life, such as tea, coffee, and tobacco? Do you retrench yourself to any inconvenience to save them? Do you daily pray for them in private? Are you laying by something to put into the treasury of the Lord when you group to pray? If you are not doing these things and if your soul is not agonized for the poor benighted heathen, why are you such a hypocrite as to pretend to be a Christian? Why, your profession is an insult to Jesus Christ!

NEGLECT OF FAMILY DUTIES

MOM, WHY DON'T I EVER SEE DADDY PRAY?

HUMPH! SOME CHRISTIAN!

WOW!

13

HOW OFTEN HAVE YOU ENTIRELY NEGLECTED TO WATCH YOUR CONDUCT, AND, HAVING BEEN OFF YOUR GUARD, HAVE SINNED BEFORE THE WORLD, AND BEFORE THE CHURCH AND BEFORE GOD!

NEGLECT TO WATCH OVER YOUR BRETHREN

WE'VE BEEN GOING HERE FOR THREE YEARS.... I GUESS IT'S TIME WE WERE INTRODUCED!

WORLDLY MINDEDNESS

LORD, THAT DOLLAR I GIVE EVERY SUNDAY IS ALL YOURS, BUT ALL THIS IS MINE!

PRIDE

UMMM — YOU HANDSOME BEAST, YOU!

14

YOU HAVE GONE CARING MORE HOW YOU APPEARED OUTWARDLY IN THE SIGHT OF MORTAL MAN...THAN HOW YOU APPEARED IN THE SIGHT OF A SOUL SEARCH-ING GOD. — WOULD YOU TAKE ALL THESE PAINS ABOUT YOUR LOOKS IF EVERY PERSON WERE BLIND?

ENVY

WHY SHOULD HE HAVE EVERYTHING?

IF YOU HAVE HARBORED THIS SPIRIT OF HELL REPENT DEEPLY BEFORE GOD OR HE'LL NEVER FORGIVE YOU.

CENSORIOUSNESS

INSTANCES WHEN YOU HAVE HAD A BITTER
SPIRIT, AND SPOKEN OF CHRISTIANS IN A
MANNER DEVOID OF CHARITY AND LOVE.

SLANDER

15

TO TELL THE TRUTH WITH THE DESIGN
TO INJURE IS SLANDER.

LEVITY

HOW OFTEN HAVE YOU
TRIFLED BEFORE GOD
AS YOU WOULD NOT HAVE
DARED TO TRIFLE IN
THE PRESENCE OF AN
EARTHLY SOVEREIGN?

LYING

"ANY SPECIES OF DESIGNED DECEPTION !"

BUT THEY WERE ONLY LITTLE WHITE LIES !

PUT THEM DOWN --- ALL OF THEM !

CHEATING

BLAH BLAH BLAH

BOSS

©!!!★! ANOTHER 20 MINUTES FOR A COFFEE BREAK !

16

SET DOWN ALL THE CASES IN WHICH YOU HAVE DEALT WITH AN INDIVIDUAL AND DONE TO HIM THAT WHICH YOU WOULD NOT LIKE TO HAVE DONE TO YOU.

HYPOCRISY

I HATE YOU ! WHY DID I EVER MARRY YOU ? YOU FAILURE !

SHUT UP ! GET READY FOR CHURCH YOU ©!!★!!

WE HAVE PEACE, PERFECT PEACE !

ROBBING GOD

BAD TEMPER

HINDERING OTHERS FROM BEING USEFUL

PERHAPS YOU HAVE WEAKENED THEIR
INFLUENCE BY INSINUATIONS AGAINST THEM

NEGLECT OF SELF DENIAL

Break up your fallow ground: for it is time to seek the Lord, till He come and rain righteousness upon you. — Hos. 10:12

To break up the fallow ground, is to break up your hearts, to prepare your minds to bring forth fruit unto God.

Go thoroughly to work in all this. Go now. Do not put it off; that will only make the matter worse. Confess **18** to God those sins that have been committed against God, and to man those sins that have been committed against man. Do not think of getting off by going round the stumbling-blocks. Take them up out of the way. In breaking up your fallow ground, you must remove every obstruction. Things may be left that you think little things, and you may wonder why you do not feel as you wish to feel in religion, when the reason is that your proud and carnal mind has covered up something which God required you to confess and remove. Break up all the ground and turn it over. Do not "balk" it, as the farmer says; do not turn aside for little difficulties; drive the plough right through them, beam deep, and turn the ground up, so that it may all be mellow and soft, and fit to receive the seed and bear fruit "an hundred-fold."

PREVAILING PRAYER

Most Christians come up to prevailing prayer by a protracted process. Their minds gradually become filled with anxiety about an object, so that they will even go about their business sighing out their desires to God. Just as the mother whose child is sick goes round her house sighing as if her heart would break. And if she is a praying mother, her sighs are breathed out to God all the day long. If she goes out of the room where her child is, her mind is still on it; and if she is asleep, still her thoughts are on it, and she starts

in her dreams, thinking that perhaps it may be dying. Her whole mind is absorbed in that sick child. This is the state of the mind in which Christians offer prevailing prayer.

20   If you mean to pray effectually, you must pray a great deal. It was said of the Apostle James that after he was dead it was found that his knees were calloused, like a camel's knees, by praying so much. Ah, here was the secret of the success of those primitive ministers! They had calloused knees!

If you intend prayer to be effectual, you must offer it in the name of Christ.

Take a fact which was related in my hearing by a minister. He said that in a certain town there had been no revival for many years; the Church was nearly extinct, the youth were all unconverted, and desolation reigned unbroken. There lived in a retired part of the town, an aged man, a blacksmith by trade, and of so stammering a tongue that it was painful to hear him speak. On one Friday, as he was at work in his shop, alone, his mind became greatly exercised about the state of the Church and of the impenitent. His agony became so great that he was induced to lay by his work, lock the shop door, and spend the afternoon in prayer.

He prevailed, and on the Lord's day called on the minister and desired him to appoint a "conference meeting." After some hesitation, the minister consented; observing however, that he feared but few would attend. He appointed it the same evening at a large private house.

When evening came, more assembled than could be accommodated in the house. All were silent for a time, until one sinner broke out in tears, and said, if any one could pray, would he pray for him? Another followed, and another, and still another, until it was found that persons from every quarter of the town were under deep conviction. And what was remarkable was, that they all dated their conviction at the hour that the old man was praying in his shop.

PRAYER OF FAITH

*THEREFORE I SAY UNTO YOU, WHAT THINGS
SOEVER YE DESIRE WHEN YE PRAY, BELIEVE THAT
YE RECEIVE THEM, AND YE SHALL HAVE THEM.*

MARK 11:24

You must first obtain evidence that God will bestow the blessing. How did Daniel make out to offer the prayer of faith? He searched the Scriptures. Now, you need not let your Bible lie on a shelf, and expect God to reveal His promises to you. "Search the Scriptures," and see where you can get either a general or special promise, or a prophecy, on which you can plant your feet. Go through your Bible, and you will find it full of such precious promises, which you may plead in faith.

22 You must persevere. You are not to pray for a thing once and then cease, and call that prayer of faith. Look at Daniel. He prayed twenty-one days, and did not cease till he had obtained the blessing. He set his heart and his face unto the Lord, to seek by prayer and supplications, with fasting, and sack-cloth, and ashes; and he held on three weeks, and then the answer came. And why did not it come before? God sent an Archangel to bear the message, but the devil hindered him all this time. See what Christ says in the Parable of the Unjust Judge, and the Parable of the Loaves. What does He teach us by them? Why, that God will grant answers to prayer when it is importunate. "Shall not God avenge His own elect, which cry day and night unto Him?" (Luke 18:7.)

DANIEL
3 WEEKS OF FASTING—PRAYER
SACKCLOTH AND ASHES

If you would pray in faith, be sure to walk every day with God. If you do, He will tell you what to pray for. Be filled with His Spirit, and He will give you objects enough to pray for. He will give you as much of the spirit of prayer as you have strength of body to bear.

He intercedes for the saints. "He maketh intercession for us," and "helpeth our infirmities," when "we know not what to pray for as we ought." He helps Christians to pray "according to the will of God." or for the things that God desires them to pray for.

The Spirit makes the Christian feel the value of souls and the guilt and danger of sinners in their present condition.

ON BEING FILLED WITH THE SPIRIT

Not because it is a matter of justice for God to give you His Spirit, but because He has promised to give His Spirit to those that ask. "If ye then, being evil, know how to give good gifts unto your children: how much more shall your heavenly Father give the Holy Spirit to them that ask Him?" (Luke 11:13.) If you ask for the Holy Spirit, God has promised to answer.

WHY MANY DO NOT HAVE THE FULLNESS OF THE SPIRIT

A HYPOCRITICAL LIFE!

THE SPIRIT OF GOD IS SOLEMN, AND SERIOUS AND WILL NOT DWELL WITH THOSE WHO GIVE WAY TO THOUGHTLESS LEVITY.

THE CONSEQUENCES OF HAVING
THE FULLNESS OF THE SPIRIT

IF YOU HAVE MUCH OF THE SPIRIT OF GOD, YOU
MUST MAKE UP YOUR MIND TO HAVE MUCH OPPOSITION
BOTH IN THE CHURCH AND THE WORLD.

OFTEN THE ELDERS AND EVEN THE MINISTER WILL
OPPOSE YOU, IF YOU ARE FILLED WITH THE SPIRIT OF GOD.

IF YOU HAVE MUCH OF THE SPIRIT OF GOD, YOU MUST EXPECT
FREQUENT AND AGONIZING CONFLICTS WITH SATAN.

BUT THE LUKEWARM, SLOTHFUL, WORLDLY MINDED
CHRISTIANS, SATAN DOESN'T BOTHER WITH

THE CONSEQUENCES OF HAVING THE FULLNESS OF THE SPIRIT

If you are filled with the Spirit of God, you must expect to feel great distress in view of the condition of the Church and of the world. Some spiritual epicures ask to be filled with the Spirit because they think He will make them so perfectly happy. Some people think that spiritual Christians are always free from sorrow. There never was a greater mistake. Read your Bibles, and see how the prophets and apostles were always groaning and distressed, in view of the state of the Church and of the world.

If you are filled with the Spirit, you will not find yourselves distressed, and galled, and worried, when people speak against you. When I find people irritated and fretting at any little thing that touches them, I am sure they have not the Spirit of Christ.

26 You will be calm under affliction; not thrown into confusion or consternation when you see the storm coming over you. People around will be astonished at your calmness and cheerfulness under heavy trials, not knowing the inward supports of those who are filled with the Spirit.

MEETINGS FOR PRAYER

IF THOSE WHO HAVE HAD HARD FEELINGS AGAINST EACH OTHER REALLY UNITE IN PRAYER — THE DIFFICULTIES WILL VANISH.

ONE BELIEVER WHO OBTAINS THE SPIRIT OF PRAYER
WILL OFTEN AROUSE AN ENTIRE CHURCH.

WHEN BELIEVERS ARE UNITED, AND PRAYING AS
THEY SHOULD, GOD OPENS THE WINDOWS OF
HEAVEN AND POURS OUT HIS BLESSINGS TIL
THERE IS NOT ROOM TO RECEIVE IT.

THE MANNER OF CONDUCTING A PRAYER MEETING

THE PERSON WHO LEADS, SHOULD
BRING THE OBJECT TO BE PRAYED
FOR DIRECTLY BEFORE THE MINDS
OF THE PEOPLE.

IF YOU CAME TO PRAY
FOR NO OBJECT IN
PARTICULAR — YOU'D
BETTER GO HOME !

LET THOSE WHO ARE MOST INCLINED TO
PRAY DO SO — WHEN EVER IT IS SAFE.

BUT OCCASIONALLY ONE OF
THESE CREEP IN.

GIVE UP THE MEETING TO THE
SPIRIT OF GOD. IF ANYTHING
NEED BE SET RIGHT — LET THE
LEADER REMARK, FREELY AND
KINDLY AND PUT IT RIGHT AND
THEN GO ON AGAIN.

CALL FIRST UPON THE MOST SPIRITUAL TO PRAY.
OTHERWISE, IF YOU CALL ON THOSE WHO ARE
COLD AND LIFELESS THEY WILL BE LIKELY TO
DIFFUSE A CHILL.

PRAYERS SHOULD BE VERY SHORT

USUALLY THOSE WHO
PRAY LONG IN A
MEETING DO SO, NOT
BECAUSE THEY ARE
SPIRITUAL ----- BUT
BECAUSE THEY ARE NOT !

"EVERY MINISTER OUGHT TO KNOW THAT IF THE PRAYER MEETINGS ARE NEGLECTED, ALL HIS LABORS ARE IN VAIN."

WHEN A CHRISTIAN IS IRRITABLE — FLIES INTO A PASSION AND GOES TO THE LAW — HE CANNOT RECOMMEND RELIGION WHILE HE HAS SUCH A SPIRIT.

30 NOTHING MAKES SO SOLEMN AN IMPRESSION UPON SINNERS, AND BEARS DOWN WITH SUCH TREMENDOUS WEIGHT ON THEIR CONSCIENCES, AS TO SEE A CHRISTIAN, TRULY CHRIST-LIKE BEARING AFFRONTS AND INJURIES WITH THE MEEKNESS OF A LAMB — IT CUTS LIKE A TWO-EDGED SWORD.

A CHRISTIAN <u>MUST</u> BE ABSOLUTELY HONEST IN <u>EVERYTHING</u>!

Not one truth in a hundred, that is preached, takes effect, because the lives of the professors declare that it is not so.

Every Christian makes an impression by his conduct, and witnesses either for one side or the other. His looks, dress, whole demeanour, make a constant impression on one side or the other. He cannot help testifying for or against religion. He is either gathering with Christ, or scattering abroad. At every step you tread on chords that will vibrate to all eternity. Every time you move, you touch keys whose sound will re-echo all over the hills and dales of heaven, and through all the dark caverns and vaults of hell. Every movement of your lives, you are exerting a tremendous influence that will tell on the immortal interests of souls all around you. Are you asleep, while all your conduct is exerting such an influence?

TO WIN SOULS REQUIRES WISDOM

BE SURE THE PERSON IS PERFECTLY SOBER!

TALK TO HIM WHEN HE IS IN A GOOD HUMOR.

NEVER INTERFERE WITH WORK—CHOOSE A TIME WHEN HE IS NOT INVOLVED IN ANY OTHER SUBJECT.

CONVERSE WITH HIM ONLY WHEN HE IS ALONE!

IF YOU HAVE A FEELING FOR A PARTICULAR INDIVIDUAL, TAKE AN OPPORTUNITY TO CONVERSE WITH THAT INDIVIDUAL WHILE THIS FEELING CONTINUES.

WHEN YOU APPROACH A
CARELESS INDIVIDUAL,
BE SURE TO TREAT HIM KINDLY

BE SOLEMN — BE
RESPECTFUL AND
BE PATIENT

GUARD YOUR OWN SPIRIT AND
TEMPER — SOME SINNERS WANT
NO BETTER TRIUMPH THAN TO
SEE YOU ANGRY.

34

DON'T TAKE A SINNER'S SIDE AGAINST ANOTHER
CHRISTIAN — IF YOU AGREE WITH HIM —
HE'LL FEEL THAT YOU ARE ON HIS SIDE.

BE SHORT AS POSSIBLE — PRESS HOME
THE FUNDAMENTAL TRUTHS

BE SURE TO PRAY WITH HIM. IF YOU CONVERSE
WITH HIM AND LEAVE HIM WITHOUT PRAYING,
YOU LEAVE YOUR WORK UNDONE.

A MINISTER HAS
THE POWERS OF HELL
TO OVERCOME — SINNERS ARE OPPOSED TO THEIR
OWN SALVATION. THE WHOLE FRAME WORK OF
SOCIETY, ALMOST, IS HOSTILE TO THE GOSPEL.

35

HE MUST UNDERSTAND HOW TO WAKE UP
THE PROFESSING CHRISTIANS, TO PREVENT
THEM FROM HINDERING THE CONVERSION
OF SINNERS — INDEED A RARE QUALIFICATION
IN THE CHRISTIAN MINISTRY

HE MUST KNOW HOW TO
SET THE CHURCH TO WORK

HE MUST SENSE WHEN THE
CHRISTIANS ARE BECOMING
PROUD OR LOSING THE SPIRIT
OF PRAYER

HE MUST PROBE AND TRY TO KEEP
THEM GATHERING IN THE HARVEST
FOR THE LORD.

☑ **HE MUST KNOW HOW TO PREACH.**

☑ **HOW TO PRAY**

☑ **HOW TO CONDUCT PRAYER MEETINGS**

☑ **HOW TO BRING GOD'S TRUTH TO BEAR AGAINST THE POWERS OF DARKNESS**

DOES NOT ALL THIS REQUIRE WISDOM?

PRAY FOR YOUR MINISTER

HOW TO PREACH THE GOSPEL

"HE THAT WINNETH SOULS IS WISE."   PROV. 11:30

In regard to the matter of preaching. (a) First, all preaching should be practical. The proper end of all doctrine is practice. Anything brought forward as doctrine, which cannot be made use of as practical, is not preaching the Gospel. There is none of that sort of preaching in the Bible. That is all practical. "All Scripture is given by inspiration of God, and is profitable for doctrine, for reproof, for correction, for instruction in righteousness: that the man of God may be perfect, throughly furnished unto all good works" (2 Tim. 3:16, 17).

Preaching should be direct. The Gospel should be preached to men, and not about men. The minister must address his hearers. He must preach to them about themselves, and not leave the impression that he is preaching to them about others. He will never do them any good, further than he succeeds in convincing each individual that he is the person in question. Many preachers seem very much afraid of making the impression that they mean anybody in particular. They are preaching against certain sins — not that these have anything to do with the sinner; they would by no means speak as if they supposed any of their hearers were guilty of these abominable practices. Now this is anything but preaching the Gospel. Thus did not the prophets, nor Christ, nor the apostles. Nor do those ministers do this, who are successful in winning souls to Christ.

If a minister means to promote a revival, he should be very careful not to introduce controversy. He will grieve away the Spirit of God.

REMARKS: *MANNER OF PREACHING*

TALK FROM THE PULPIT AS YOU WOULD IN PRIVATE CONVERSATION.

AVOID THE LOFTY SWELLING STYLE. IT MAKES SINNERS FEEL THAT RELIGION IS SOME MYSTERIOUS THING.

USE WORDS THAT CAN BE PERFECTLY UNDERSTOOD. DO NOT, FOR FEAR OF APPEARING UNLEARNED, USE LANGUAGE WHICH PEOPLE DO NOT UNDERSTAND.

Preaching should be parabolical. That is, illustrations should be constantly used, drawn from incidents, real or supposed. Jesus Christ constantly illustrated His instructions in this way. He would either advance a principle and then illustrate it by a parable — that is, a short story of some event, real or imaginary — or else He would bring out the principle in the parable. There are millions of facts that can be used to advantage, and yet very few ministers dare to use them, for fear somebody will reproach them. "Oh," says somebody, "he actually tells stories!" Tells stories! Why that is the way Jesus Christ preached. And it is the only way to preach.

I know, in fact, that men of the first minds often get ideas they never had before, from illustrations which were designed to bring the Gospel down to the comprehension of a child. Such men are commonly so occupied with the affairs of this world, that they do not think much on the subject of religion, and they therefore need the plainest preaching, and they will like it.

What is the dignity of the pulpit? What an idea, to see a minister go into the pulpit to sustain its dignity! Alas, alas! During my foreign tour, I heard an English missionary preach exactly in that way. I believe he was a good man, and out of the pulpit he would talk like a man who meant what he said. But no sooner was he in the pulpit than he appeared like a perfect automaton — swelling, mouthing, and singing, enough to put **38** all the people to sleep. And the difficulty seemed to be that he wanted to maintain the dignity of the pulpit.

It is objected that this preaching is theatrical. The Bishop of London once asked Garrick, the celebrated actor, why it was that actors, in representing a mere fiction, should move an assembly, even to tears, while ministers, in representing the most solemn realities, could scarcely obtain a hearing. The philosophical Garrick well replied: "It is because we represent fiction as reality, and you represent reality as a fiction."

Now, what is the objection to all this in preaching? The actor suits the action to the word, and the word to the action. His looks, his hands, his attitudes, and everything, are designed to express the full meaning of the writer. Now, this should be the aim of the preacher. And if by "theatrical" be meant the strongest possible representation of the sentiments expressed, then the more theatrical the sermon is, the better. And if ministers are too stiff, and the people too fastidious, to learn even from an actor, or from the stage, the method of swaying mind, enforcing sentiment, and diffusing the warmth of burning thought over a congregation, then they must go on with their prosing, and reading, and sanctimonious starch. But let them remember, that while they are thus turning away and decrying the art of the actor, and attempting to support the "dignity of the pulpit," the theatres can be thronged every night. The common sense of the people will be entertained with that manner of speaking, and sinners will go down to hell.

WHEN THERE IS A VACANCY FOR A MINISTER, USUALLY TWO POINTS ARE CONSIDERED . . .

(1) IS HE POPULAR? (2) HE SHOULD BE LEARNED

BUT THE MOST IMPORTANT ISSUE OF ALL IS . . .

"IS HE WISE TO WIN SOULS?"

IF HE HAS NOT THIS ABILITY, YOUR CHILDREN AND NEIGHBORS WILL BE IN GREAT DANGER UNDER HIS PREACHING.

HOW CAN CHURCHES HELP MINISTERS?

THINGS THAT MUST BE AVOIDED

By all means keep clear of the idea, both in theory and practice, that a minister alone is to promote revivals. Many professing Christians are inclined to take a passive attitude on this subject, and feel as if they had nothing to do. They have employed a minister, and paid him to feed them with instructions and comfort, and now they have nothing to do but to sit and swallow the food he gives. They are to pay his salary and attend on his preaching — and they think that is doing a great deal. And he, on his part, is expected to preach good, sound comfortable doctrine, to bolster them up, and make them feel comfortable. So, they expect to go to heaven. I tell you THEY WILL GO TO HELL if this is their religion! That is not the way to heaven.

Rest assured that where this spirit prevails in the Church, however good the minister may be, the Church has taken the course to prevent a revival. Be the minister ever so faithful, ever so devoted, ever so talented and eloquent, though he may wear himself out, and perhaps destroy his life, he will have little or no revival.

THAT IS JUST AS ABSURD AS A MINISTER FIGHTING FOR THE CAUSE OF CHRIST, WITHOUT THE SUPPORT OF HIS CHURCH.

40

DO NOT CALL THE PREACHING "TOO PLAIN" SIMPLY BECAUSE IT EXPOSES THE FAULTS OF THE CHURCH

PRAY THAT THE TRUTH MAY COME DOWN ON THE UNGODLY LIKE FIRE!...CHRIST CAN GET ALONG VERY WELL WITHOUT THEIR MONEY!

DON'T WASTE THE MINISTER'S TIME...
IT'S MORE PRECIOUS THAN GOLD!

DON'T HINDER THE PASTOR — GIVE HIM A DECENT
SALARY — HIS JOB IS TOUGH ENOUGH

PAY HIM A SALARY WITHOUT BEING ASKED!

THIS MOMENT COULD BE THE MOST IMPORTANT MOMENT OF YOUR LIFE!

WAAAAAAAAH!

IF CHILDREN WEEP, THEY SHOULD BE INSTANTLY REMOVED.

PRAY FOR YOUR MINISTER. EVEN THE APOSTLES USED TO URGE THE CHURCHES TO PRAY FOR THEM THIS IS MORE IMPORTANT THAN YOU CAN IMAGINE.

HINDERANCES TO REVIVALS

A REVIVAL WILL STOP WHENEVER THE CHURCH BELIEVES IT IS GOING TO CEASE.

42

I GIVE THE REVIVAL ABOUT TWO MORE WEEKS!

THAT'S ABOUT WHAT I FIGURED!

WHENEVER THE FRIENDS OF REVIVALS BEGIN TO PROPHESY THAT THE REVIVAL IS GOING TO STOP, THEY SHOULD BE <u>INSTANTLY</u> REBUKED IN THE NAME OF THE LORD.

✓ IT WILL CEASE WHEN CHRISTIANS BECOME MECHANICAL IN THEIR ATTEMPTS TO PROMOTE IT.

✓ IT WILL CEASE WHEN THE CHURCH PREFERS TO ATTEND TO SELFISH CONCERNS, RATHER THAN GOD'S BUSINESS.

✓ IT WILL CEASE WHEN CHRISTIANS GET PROUD OF THEIR REVIVAL

THE REVIVAL WILL CEASE WHENEVER CHRISTIANS GET THE IDEA THAT THE WORK WILL GO ON WITHOUT THEIR AID.

WHEN CHRISTIANS BEGIN TO PROSELYTIZE AND
MAKE EFFORTS TO GET CONVERTS TO JOIN THEIR
CHURCH... YOU WILL SEE THE END OF REVIVAL

ONE SURE WAY TO KILL A REVIVAL.
THE SPIRIT IS GRIEVED AWAY.

WHEN CHRISTIANS ARE IN THE SPIRIT OF REVIVAL
THEY AFFECTIONATELY CALL EACH OTHER
BROTHER AND SISTER...

BUT WHEN THEY LOSE THE SPIRIT OF BROTHERLY LOVE,
THE SPIRIT OF GOD IS GRIEVED AND THE POWER OF GOD
IS WITHDRAWN.

The revival will stop when the Church gets exhausted by labour. Multitudes of Christians commit a great mistake here in time of revival. They are so thoughtless, and have so little judgment, that they will break up all their habits of living, neglect to eat and sleep at the proper hours, and let the excitement run away with them, so that they overdo their bodies, and are so imprudent that they soon become exhausted, and it is impossible for them to continue in the work. Revivals often cease from negligence and imprudence, in this respect, on the part of those engaged in carrying them on, and declensions follow.

✔ When the Church, in any way, grieves the Holy Spirit.

✔ When Christians refuse to render to the Lord according to the benefits received.

✔ Slandering revivals will often put them down.

✔ If the Church wishes to promote revivals, she must sanctify the Lord's day.

✔ A revival will cease when the Church begins to speculate about abstract doctrines.

A revival will decline and cease, unless Christians are frequently re-dedicated. By this I mean, that Christians, in order to keep in the spirit of revival, commonly need to be frequently convicted, and humbled and broken down before God, and "re-dedicated." This is something which many do not understand, when we talk about a Christian being re-dedicated. But the fact is, that in a revival, the Christian's heart is liable to get crusted over, and lose its exquisite relish for Divine things; his unction and prevalence in prayer abate, and then he must be dedicated over again. It is impossible to keep him in such a state as not to do injury to the work, unless he passes through such a process every few days. I have never laboured in revivals in company with any one who would keep in the work and be fit to manage a revival continually, who did not pass through this process of breaking down as often as once in two or three weeks.

OH FATHER, I FEEL MYSELF PULLING AWAY FROM YOU --- PLEASE FORGIVE ME!

46 But whenever Satan succeeds in absorbing public attention in any other subject, he will put an end to the revival. No matter what the subject is.

In one place where there was a revival, certain ministers formed a combination against the pastor of the Church, and a plan was set on foot to ruin him, and they actually got him prosecuted before his Presbytery, and had a trial that lasted six weeks, right in the midst of the revival; but the work still went

REGARDLESS OF THE CONFUSION ABOUT YOU---HOLD FAST IN PRAYER!

on. The praying members of the Church laid themselves out so in the work, that it continued triumphantly throughout the whole scene. The pastor was called off, to attend his trial, but there was another minister that laboured among the people, and the members did not even go to the trial, but kept praying and labouring for souls, and the revival rode out the storm. In many places, opposition has risen up in the Church, but a few humble souls have kept at their work, and our gracious God has **47** stretched out His naked arm and made the revival go forward in spite of all opposition.

THE CHURCH MUST BE AGREED.

Oh, if we could find but one Church perfectly and heartily agreed in all these points, so that they could pray and labour together, all as one, what good would be done! Oh, what do Christians think, how can they keep still, when God has brought down His blessings so that if any two were agreed as touching the things they ask for it would be done? Alas! alas! how bitter will be the remembrance of the janglings in the Church, when Christians come to see the crowds of lost souls that have gone down to hell because we were not agreed to labour and pray for their salvation.

48

FALSE COMFORT FOR SINNERS

The great design of dealing with an anxious sinner is to clear up all his difficulties and darkness, do away with all his errors, sap the foundation of his selfrighteous hopes, and sweep away every vestige of comfort that he can find in himself. There is often much difficulty in all this, and much instruction is required. Sinners often cling with a death-grasp to their false dependence. The last place to which a sinner ever betakes himself for relief is to Jesus Christ. Sinners had rather be saved in any other way in the world. They had rather make any sacrifice, go to any expense, or endure any suffering, than just throw themselves as guilty and lost rebels upon Christ alone for salvation. This is the very last way in which they are ever willing to be saved. It cuts up all their self-righteousness, and annihilates their pride and self-satisfaction so completely that they are exceedingly unwilling to adopt it.

WHY MILLIONS ARE NOW IN HELL

DO I HAVE TO CONFORM TO THE HUMILIATION OF THE GOSPEL ?-I NEED PITY AND COMFORT, I SHUDDER AT THE THOUGHT OF HELL

THE POOR GUY

FORGET IT FOR THE TIME BEING!

I GUESS IT ISN'T VERY IMPORTANT THEN ! I'LL FORGET THE WHOLE THING !

I WONDER IF I SAID SOMETHING WRONG ?

THE DANGEROUS CHRISTIAN WHO GIVES FALSE COMFORT

THE ANXIOUS SINNER

50

GOD HAS MORE BENEVOLENCE AND COMPASSION THAN ALL MEN

GOD WILL NOT ALTER. HE KNOWS THAT NOTHING WILL MAKE THE SINNER HAPPY, UNTIL HE REPENTS OF HIS SINS AND FORSAKES THEM AND TURNS TO GOD.

ERRORS MADE IN PRAYING FOR SINNERS

Praying for them as "poor sinners." Does the Bible ever use such language as this? The Bible never speaks of them as "poor sinners," as if they deserved to be pitied more than blamed. Christ pities sinners in His heart. And so does God pity them. He feels in His heart all the gushings of compassion for them, when He sees them going on, obstinate and wilfull in gratifying their own lusts, as the peril of His eternal wrath. But He never lets an impression escape from Him, as if the sinner were just a "poor creature" — to be pitied, as if he could not help his position. The idea that he is poor, rather than wicked; unfortunate, rather than guilty, relieves the sinner greatly. I have seen the sinner writhe with agony under the truth, in a meeting, until somebody began to pray for him as a "poor" creature. And then he would gush out into tears, and weep profusely, and think he was greatly benefited by such a prayer, saying: "Oh, what a good prayer that was!" If you go now and converse with that sinner, you will probably find that he is still pitying himself as a poor unfortunate creature — perhaps even weeping over his unhappy condition; but his conviction of sin, his deep impressions of awful guilt, are all gone.

DIRECTIONS TO SINNERS

WHAT MUST I DO TO BE SAVED? ACTS 16:30

IMPROPER DIRECTIONS

No direction should be given that does not include a change of heart, or a right heart, or hearty obedience to Christ. In other words, nothing is proper which does not imply actually becoming a Christian.

A PROPER ANSWER

His great object in striving with them is, to dislodge them from their hiding-places, and bring them to submit to God at once.

EXPLAIN IT, I'M CONFUSED!

✓ YOU MUST REPENT AND HATE SIN.

✓ LOVE GOD SUPREMELY

✓ BELIEVE THE GOSPEL

CHOOSE THIS DAY WHOM YOU WILL SERVE

EXPLAIN WHAT YOU DO NOT MEAN TO AVOID CONFUSION

POSSIBLE ERRORS IN WHICH ANXIOUS SINNERS ARE APT TO FALL

52

FIRST OF ALL, I WILL MAKE MYSELF BETTER!

NO! SIMPLY ACCEPT SALVATION

I MUST WAIT FOR DIFFERENT FEELINGS BEFORE I SUBMIT

IT IS NOT A QUESTION OF FEELING, BUT OF WILLINGNESS AND ACTION!

AM I TO BELIEVE IN CHRIST BEFORE MY HEART IS CHANGED?

YES! DO NOT WAIT! WHEN YOU REPENT, BELIEVE AND LOVE GOD, YOUR HEART WILL BE CHANGED.

Much depends on the manner of which a person is dealt with when under conviction. Much of his future comfort and usefulness depends on the clearness, strength, and firmness with which the directions of the Gospel are given, when he is under conviction. If those who deal with him are afraid to use the probe thoroughly, he will always be a poor, sickly, doubting Christian. The true mode is to deal thoroughly and plainly with the sinner, to tear away every excuse he can offer, and to show him plainly what he is and what he ought to be:

So far as I have had opportunity to observe, those persons with whom conversion was most sudden have commonly turned out to be the best Christians.

INSTRUCTIONS TO CONVERTS

FEED MY LAMBS ... JOHN 21:15

THE HOPES OF YOUNG CONVERTS:

It is a great evil, ordinarily, to encourage persons to hope they are Christians. Very likely you may judge prematurely. Or if not, it is better, in any case, that they should find it out for themselves — that is, supposing they do not see it at once.

When persons express hope, and yet express doubts, too, it is generally because the work in not thorough.

YOUNG CONVERTS SHOULD OFFER THEMSELVES TO SOME FUNDAMENTAL CHURCH IMMEDIATELY.

THINGS WHICH SHOULD NOT BE TAUGHT

GREAT EVIL HAS BEEN DONE BY THE PRACTICE OF KEEPING PERSONS OUT OF THE CHURCH TOO LONG A TIME IN ORDER TO SEE IF THEY WERE CHRISTIANS

ARE YOU SURE YOU'RE NOT A DRUNKARD?

HOW DO YOU KNOW IF YOU'RE REALLY SAVED?

ARE YOU SURE YOU'LL BE ABLE TO HOLD OUT??

ALL I WANT TO DO IS WORSHIP THE LORD!

JESUS CHRIST SAYS TO HIS CHURCH: "HERE, TAKE THESE LAMBS, AND FEED THEM AND SHELTER THEM AND WATCH OVER THEM AND PROTECT THEM."

JUST WAIT!

OHH, I'M SO HAPPY IN THE LORD!

YOU WON'T ALWAYS FEEL THIS WAY---

SOON YOU'LL BE AS COLD AS WE ARE

SHAME!!
JUST PREPARING THE YOUNG CONVERT TO EXPECT THAT HE WILL BACKSLIDE AS A MATTER OF COURSE.

THINGS WHICH ARE IMPORTANT SHOULD BE TAUGHT

"YE ARE NOT YOUR OWN" 1 COR. 6:19

YOUNG CONVERTS SHOULD BE TAUGHT TO RENOUNCE OWNERSHIP OF ALL THEIR POSSESSIONS AND TO THEMSELVES

IF I COULD ONLY BE LIKE HIM!

NO! — KEEP YOUR EYES ON CHRIST!

THEY SHOULD ALWAYS LOOK AT CHRIST AS THEIR MODEL.

IT IS TIME CHRISTIANS WERE MADE ACTUALLY TO FEEL THAT THEY HAVE NO INTEREST WHATEVER, SEPARATE FROM THE INTERESTS OF JESUS CHRIST AND HIS KINGDOM.

NOW THAT I'M SAVED, I'LL SING HYMNS, RELAX AND WAIT FOR THE LORD!

SUCH WAS NOT THE TEMPER OF THE APOSTLES: THEY TRAVAILED FOR SOULS; THEY LABORED IN WEARINESS AND PAINFULNESS, AND WERE "IN DEATHS OFT" TO SAVE SINNERS.

CAREFUL, DON'T REBUKE HIM, IT CAN BECOME A DANGEROUS HABIT!

ZZZZZZZ

KEEP YOUNG CONVERTS FROM CENSORING OLD BELIEVERS WHO ARE COLD AND DEAD --- THIS HABIT WILL POISON THEIR MINDS AND DESTROY THEIR RELIGION.

YOUNG CONVERTS MUST LEARN TO SAY NO!

¡NO!

COME ON BACK TO US!

YOU'RE GOING THE WRONG WAY

ONCE THE ICE IS BROKEN — HE GIVES IN THEN HE BECOMES ONE OF THEM AGAIN.

HOW THE CHURCH SHOULD TREAT YOUNG CONVERTS

56

They should be watched over by the Church, and warned of their dangers, just as a tender mother watches over her young children. Young converts do not know at all the dangers by which they are surrounded. The devices of the devil, the temptations of the world, the power of their own passions and habits, and the thousand forms of danger, they do not know; and if not properly watched and warned, they will run right into such dangers.

Be tender in reproving them. When Christians find it necessary to reprove young converts, they should be exceedingly careful in their manner of doing it. Young converts should be faithfully watched over by the elder members of the Church, and when they begin to lose ground, or to turn aside, they should be promptly admonished, and, if necessary, reproved. But to do it in a wrong manner is worse than to do it at all.

If the Church had only done her duty in training up young converts to work and labour for Christ, the world would have been converted long ago. But instead of this, how many Churches actually oppose young converts who attempt to set themselves to work for Christ.

THE BACKSLIDER IN HEART

EVIDENCES OF A BACKSLIDDEN HEART

- ✔ Neglect of Family Prayer
- ✔ Religious Apathy
- ✔ Loving Worldly Entertainment
- ✔ No Interest In Missions Or Missionary Work
- ✔ Lack Of Interest In Secret Prayer
- ✔ A Censorious Spirit
- ✔ Lax Principles in Morality
- ✔ An Irritable, Uncontrolled Temper
- ✔ Lack Of Interest In The Bible
- ✔ Lack of Interest In The Conversions Of Souls

- A Loss Of Interest In The Conversation And Fellowship Of Highly Spiritual People

- If You Do Not Enjoy The Service Of God

- Prevalence Of The Fear Of Man Is An Evidence Of A Backslidden Heart

- Absence From Prayer Meetings For Slight Reasons

- A sticklishness about forms, ceremonies, and non-essentials, gives evidence of a backslidden heart.

I am satisfied that the most common occasion of backsliding in heart is to be found in the clamour for indulgence of the various appetites and propensies. The appetite for food is frequently, and perhaps more frequently than any other, the occasion of backsliding. Few Christians, I fear, apprehend any danger in this direction. God's injunction is: "Whether therefore ye eat, or drink, or whatsoever ye do, do all to the glory of God" (I Cor. 10:31). Christians forget this, and eat and drink to please themselves, consulting their appetites instead of the laws of life and health. More persons are ensnared by their tables than the Church is aware of. The table is a snare of death to multitudes that no man can number. A great many people who avoid alcoholic drinks altogether, will indulge in tea and coffee, and even tobacco, and in food that, both in quantity and quality, violates every law of health. They seem to have no other law than that of appetite, and this they so deprave by abuse that, to indulge it, is to ruin body and soul together. Show me a gluttonous professor, and I will show you a backslider.

58

THE CONSEQUENCES OF A BACKSLIDING HEART

✔ FILLED WITH HIS OWN PREJUDICES ✔ FULL OF HIS OWN MISTAKES ✔ FILLED WITH HIS OWN WORDS

He will be full of his own trials. Instead of keeping out of temptation, he will run right into it. He will bring upon himself multitudes of trials that he never would have had, had he not departed from God.

The backslider in heart shall be full of his own follies. Having rejected the Divine guidance, he will evidently fall into the depths of his own foolishness. He will evidently say and do multitudes of foolish and ridiculous things. Being a professor of religion, these things will be all the more noticed. And of course bring him all the more into ridicule and contempt. A backslider is, indeed, the most foolish person in the world.

HOW TO RECOVER FROM A STATE OF BACKSLIDING

Repent at once, and do your first works over again.

Do not attempt to get back, by reforming your mere outside conduct. Begin with your heart, and at once set yourself right with God.

Do not imagine yourself to be in a justified state, for you know you are not. Your conscience condemns you, and you know that God ought to condemn you, and if He justified you in your present state, your conscience could not justify Him. Come, then, to Christ at once, like a guilty, condemned sinner, as you are; own up, and take all the shame and blame to yourself, and believe that notwithstanding all your wanderings, from God, He loves you still — that He has loved you with an everlasting love, and, therefore, with lovingkindness is drawing you.

GROWTH IN GRACE

EVIDENCES OF THE GROWTH IN GRACE

✔ JOYFULNESS UNDER CROSSES AND DISAPPOINTMENTS AND SEVERE PAIN

✔ A GROWING JEALOUSY FOR THE HONOR OF GOD FOR THE PURITY AND HONOR OF HIS CHURCH

✔ A GROWING DEADNESS TO THE FLATTERY OR CENSURE OF MEN

✔ LOSING MORE AND MORE THE CONSCIOUSNESS OF SELF

✔ LESS TEMPTATION TO RESENTMENT

✔ AN INCREASING DEADNESS TO ALL THE WORLD HAS TO OFFER

✔ BEING LESS AND LESS DISPOSED TO SPEAK SEVERELY OR TO JUDGE UNCHARITABLY OF OTHERS

✔ LESS TEMPTATION TO REMEMBER AN INJURY

✔ A GROWING TRANQUILLITY UNDER SUDDEN AND CRUSHING DISASTERS

Remember that every step of progress must be made by faith, and not by works. If you would grow in grace you must do it through faith. You must pray in faith for the filling of the Holy Spirit. You must appropriate and put on Christ through the Holy Spirit. At every forward step in your progress, you must have a fresh anointing of the Holy Spirit through faith.

REMARKS: *(FINNEY)*

The Theological Seminaries need to pay vastly more attention to growth in grace of their students. They need a professor of experimental religion, who has experience and power enough to press them along into those higher regions of Christian experience which are essential to their being able to lead the Church on to victory. It is amazing to see how little effort is made to cultivate the heart of young men studying for the ministry. We must have a change in this respect. A much higher standard of Christian experience must be required as a condition of ordination.

Is it any wonder that the Church of God is so feeble and inefficient, while the leaders and teachers are, many of them, mere children in spiritual knowledge, while a ripe Christian experience is made no part of the indispensable education of a minister? Why, this is infinitely more dangerous and ridiculous than to entrust men to lead an army in the field, while they merely understand mathematics, and never have had any training or experience in military matters.

In this respect, too, there must be a great change. Churches should refuse to ordain and receive pastors, unless they are fully satisfied of their having made much progress in Christian experience, so as to be able to lead on, and keep the Church awake.

You now know the key to revival— you have just read the words of Charles G. Finney, one of God's greatest revivalists, who a century ago, under the power of God, led thousands of souls to Christ.

Conditions were the same then as they are now. PORE OVER THIS BOOK, TALK ABOUT IT, PASS IT ON TO OTHERS— Revival is in the wind, GOD'S SPIRIT is about to be poured out upon the earth. There is the sound of the abundance of rain! Jesus commands us to BE ZEALOUS AND REPENT. Fill your lamps with oil!—

OUR KING IS COMING!

The fields are white unto harvest, the night is almost upon us and YOU are holding back the great revival.

<u>This</u> is the hour for Christ's overcomers to MOVE!

REPENT — PRAY

AND WATCH THE MIGHTY HAND
OF GOD SWEEP OUR LAND

THIS IS THE LAST CALL!

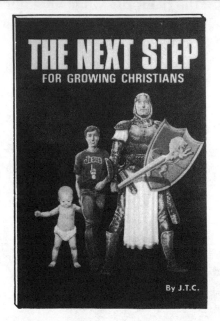